THE CHOCOLATE SUITE

by Antonio Ciacca

Project managers: Giusy Magrì and Seton Hawkins
Graphic designer: Alexander Grandi Ventura
Produced by Giusy Magrì for TwinsMusic Enterprises Corporation
Photo Cover by Karl Giant

Copyright © 2011 by TwinsMusic Enterprises Corporation.
ISBN 978-0-9828249-9-3
All rights reserved. No part of this work may be reproduced or transmitted in any form or by any means, electronic or mechanical, including photocopying or recording, or by any information storage and retrieval system, except as may be expressly permitted by the 1976 Copyright Act, or in writing from the publisher.
Library of Congress Cataloguing in Publication Data.

Table of Content

Preface	*p. 4*
Antonio Ciacca Biography	*p. 5*
Michel Richart Biography	*p. 8*
Jazz and Chocolate	*p. 9*
Chocolate # 1: "Santondino Chocomac"	*p.11*
Movement I: "Santondino"	*p.12*
Chocolate # 2: "Venezuela"	*p.14*
Movement II: "Ciacca 5"	*p.15*
Chocolate # 3: " Jazz in St. Germain"	*p.17*
Movement III: "Jobim"	*p.18*
Chocolate # 4: "Petit Richart"	*p.21*
Movement IV: "Besame Lucio"	*p.22*
Chocolate # 5: " Spice Chocomac"	*p. 25*
Movement V: " Scotty"	*p. 26*

Preface

Antonio Ciacca's Chocolate Suite draws its inspiration from the creations of master chocolatier Michel Richart, whose latest confections serve as the launching point for Ciacca's jazz suite.

Composed for the Setai Fifth Avenue Hotel to be performed at a special pairing of Richart's chocolates with music, Ciacca's Chocolate Suite comprises five movements, each inspired by one of the chocolates created for the event. The evening features a presentation by Michel Richart on the "global flavors"—the intangible qualities as perceived by the taste buds and sense of smell, and uniquely interpreted by each taster—of each chocolate, followed by a tasting complemented with discussion and music. Ciacca's original pieces help to underscore the moods and flavors of each chocolate, while building a complete experience for the tasters.

To that end, we are including the tasting notes for each chocolate below, and matching them with the corresponding musical movement. While the Chocolate Suite exists as a stand-alone work, we have included this information should you wish to repeat the tasting experiment at home.

This event is truly an experience that touches all five senses: the sight of the band and the chocolate, the sound of music and discussion, the smell of the cocoa and spices, and the tactile sensation of holding the chocolate and the music book. In that way, we share Michel Richart's vision of ensuring that the chocolate achieves the finest tasting experience for each guest, one that delights all five senses.

Seton Hawkins

Antonio Ciacca
Pianist, Composer, Arranger, Educator

Biography

"At the heart of any true jazzman is the ability to tell his own musical stories in his own way, and hopefully touch a few hearts along the way. Down in his heart, there's a song he can feel, something that no one can steal. It's his own tune, all and in part. Pianist Antonio Ciacca dances to the unique songs in his heart."
– Todd Barkan, Jazz at Lincoln Center and Record Producer

Born in Germany, raised in Italy and educated in the United States, Ciacca is able to move as fluidly among those varied cultural environments as he does between his life as a performer, composer, father of five, and top-tier arts presenter. Notably, Ciacca has served as Artistic Director for the Italian cultural agency, C-Jam, and in 2007, landed a plum job as the Director of Programming for Jazz at Lincoln Center, the impetus for his move that year from Bologna, Italy to New York City.

Ciacca began his career as a sideman for such acclaimed jazz artists as Art Farmer, James Moody, Lee Konitz, Jonny Griffin, Mark Murphy, Dave Liebman, and Steve Grossman, who he cites as his mentor, and with whom he studied for three years beginning in 1990. In 1993, he moved to Detroit to study at Wayne State University with Kenny Barron, after which he studied privately with Mingus' pianist Jackie Byard in New York. While living in Detroit, he was first exposed to gospel music, which so impressed him with its passion and energy that he soon integrated it into his own developing style as a composer and performer; he eventually went on to produce a CD for the Detroit Gospel Singers.

One of the most important events in Ciacca's career was an invitation to join the legendary saxophonist Steve Lacy's quartet in 1997; he continued to perform with Lacy for seven years. Another key encounter that would have long lasting musical and professional repercussions for Ciacca took place in 1997. "Wynton Marsalis was performing in Italy with Elvin Jones, who is my son's godfather. I'd first seen him at the Bologna Jazz Festival in 1989, and he really first opened my eyes to jazz then. But when I first saw him, I had no idea we'd ever work together." Ciacca first performed with Wynton in Wess Anderson's sextet at New York's Village Vanguard in 2004.

In 1998 he also began to perform with saxophonist Benny Golson, with whom he continues to collaborate. In 1995, Ciacca recorded his first CD as a leader, *Driemoty*, which was released on the label C-Jam. In 1999 he recorded in New York City *Hollis Avenue* for the German label YVP. In 2002, he recorded *Autumn in New York* for the Italian label Splash.

After returning to Italy, Ciacca performed throughout Europe, including an intense series of performances in London in 2003, which included appearances at Ronnie Scott's, the Royal Festival Hall Foyer, the National Theatre and the London Jazz Festival, with "The Monk Liberation Front" project, a six hour-long performance that involved thirteen musicians alternately playing Monk's unedited music—The Guardian called out Ciacca's performance as "terrific." After opening for Wynton Marsalis' concerts in Italy, in 2004 Ciacca returned to New York to again perform at the Village Vanguard with his own quartet, featuring renowned saxophonist Wess Anderson, subsequently touring with them throughout the US, UK, and Italy until 2005.

In Italy in 2004, Ciacca recorded a trio project, *Ugly Beauty* with the late Dennis Irwin and Detroit mate Ali Jackson for the legendary Italian label Soul Note, which he supported with a European tour.

In 2007, Ciacca's extensive music industry experience and comprehensive artistic vision led to his being tapped to take on the position of Director of Programming at Jazz at Lincoln Center, where he worked closely with JALC Artistic Director Wynton Marsalis until June 2011.

That same year, he met Jana Herzen, founder of Motéma Music, at a performance at the Historic Langston Hughes House in Harlem, an intimate brownstone parlor performance space that is sponsored in part by the label. Herzen offered use of the Fazioli piano at the Hughes House to Ciacca for his rehearsal needs, and over the next few weeks she took so well to Ciacca's playing and compositions that the current recording deal was initiated.

The release of *Rush Life* coincided with many changes and developments at Motéma and in the jazz industry in general. The CD represented the label's first digital-only release in the US; the project is available at download services throughout the world as well as via Motéma's own jazz portal in the US, www.motema.com. It was also one of the first Motéma projects to be sold Europe-wide through Motéma's new distribution partner, the German-based Membran. Nancy Ann-Lee, writing in the *Jazz & Blues Report*, observed, "This superb recording demonstrates Ciacca's immersion in the language of jazz".

In 2009 Ciacca turned 40. His year long celebrations included: an appearance at New York Blue Note, one week engagement at Dizzy's, performances at the Rochester and Detroit International Jazz Festivals, European Tour with special guests George Garzone and Joe Locke, release of his first music book, *The Music of Antonio Ciacca Vol. 1* and his first year teaching the course "Business of Jazz" at Julliard.

And performing at the Detroit International Jazz Festival was the climax of a fantastic journey started in Detroit in 1993 when Antonio first touched US soil. In the same year Antonio was invited to celebrate Art Tatum's Centennial and John Hendrix joined him as special guest.

In 2010 Ciacca released *Lagos Blues*, his second recording with Motéma. In two months this album became a rare gift to the jazz world, documenting for the first time the pure joy of be-bop, gospel, and blues-influenced pianist/composer Antonio Ciacca's deep long-term musical relationship with sax legend Steve Grossman. Grossman, who rose to fame in the 1970s through incendiary and groundbreaking sessions with Miles Davis, joined Ciacca's deft ensemble (Stacy Dillard, Kengo Nakamura & Ulysses Owens) to swing with impeccable style on this historic disc.

In September 2010 The Antonio Ciacca Trio performed in a special tribute to Bud Powell, which also featured The Jacky Terrason Trio, Barry Harris and Bertha Hope. In the autumn of 2010, Antonio Ciacca with TwinsMusic Enterprises curated the Second Annual *Italian Jazz Days*, showcasing the rich jazz heritage of Italy through a series of concerts featuring American and Italian Jazz artists, including among others, Joe Lovano with the Antonio Ciacca Quintet.

Currently the New York-based pianist and composer Ciacca enjoys his work as a teacher at Juilliard School, as Artist-in-Residence at the Bar On Fifth in the Setai Fifth Avenue Hotel in New York City, and as a highly sought-after performer at venues throughout the world. Ciacca plays with a rare blend of earthiness, fire, and intellect, with elements of Wynton Kelly, Red Garland, and Bobby Timmons that recall the most creatively vital and yet oddly neglected schools of jazz.

In October 2011, Ciacca served as the headline artist during a week-long tenure at Dizzy's Club Coca-Cola as a part of the Third Annual *Italian Jazz Days*. In a series of concerts entitled *The Italian-American Songbook*, Ciacca led ensembles featuring jazz luminaries including John Patitucci, George Garzone, Lewis Nash, and Dominick Farinacci.

Michel Richart
Chocolatier

Biography

Born into a chocolate-loving family, Michel Richart spent his childhood with his chocolatier father and his mother in a laboratory and chocolate shop established on the slopes of the *Croix-Rousse* in Lyon. Richart's father passed on to him his knowledge and his industry know how. Growing up, Richart learned the art of making chocolate and became conscious of the importance of the quality of raw materials, of the generosity of recipes, and of the expert precision required for every product. He perfected his art through meticulous tastings of meals, pastries, chocolates, and wines, all of which took place within the family.

Richart took over the family business from 1968 until 1985 and transformed it into a high-end *chocolaterie,* for which he received the "*Chocolaterie*" Blue Ribbon" seven times. Between 1986 and 1987, he created the concept of "Design and Chocolate" and launched the "Richart Design and Chocolate" brand. In 1988, he inaugurated his boutique in Paris, sparking what would become a worldwide phenomenon and earn his works the accolade of the "haute couture of chocolates."

Since then, Richart has opened fifteen outlets in major cities throughout the world. In 2003, he renewed his concept by creating new chocolates and regrouping them into seven aromatic families. In the newly conceived boutiques, Richart customers get to sample different flavorful notes with the help of a "chocolates organ" before proceeding to the aroma wall for their final selection.

Michel Richart credits his success to the enlightened attitudes and discerning taste buds of chocolate devotees, who are the only real guarantee of preserving the high quality of this divine treat.

JAZZ AND CHOCOLATE

During the event, Michel Richart explains his concept of the "global flavor" of chocolates. In a nutshell, these flavors are usually defined as the distinctive, intangible qualities of a particular food or drink as perceived by the taste buds and the sense of smell.

Richart, in its approach to tasting, tries to complete this with how one's memories, feelings, and experiences can enrich each chocolate's flavor—making it global—to reach optimal sensation. A truly multi-sensory experience in tasting chocolate, one that lets feelings and memories in, is one in which the taster achieves maximum pleasure.

Jazz, because of its universal, cross-cultural, impressionistic, and free form is a perfect companion for a chocolate tasting.

The global flavor, this holy grail of tasting, is therefore reached when the listener/taster is overwhelmed with pleasure due to a chocolate that follows the mood of the music, and vice versa.

Santodino Chocomac

(A hybrid between chocolate and a French macaroon)

Feelings, mood: Power, character, authority, depth, harmony, energy

Main ingredients: sugar, cream and butter from Bresse, fleur de sal, 73% cocoa from Venezuela

Sensory analysis: Essentially sweet with a hint of bitterness, caramel, dairy aromas and cocoa. Tender, soft, melting and flowing texture. Can evoke thoughts of childhood, rewards, old friends, desserts

"Global flavor": Tranquility, safety, softness, generosity, confidence, protection.

Santondino

Medium " Mambo groove"

Music by Antonio Ciacca

A Intro solo piano 8 bars

B

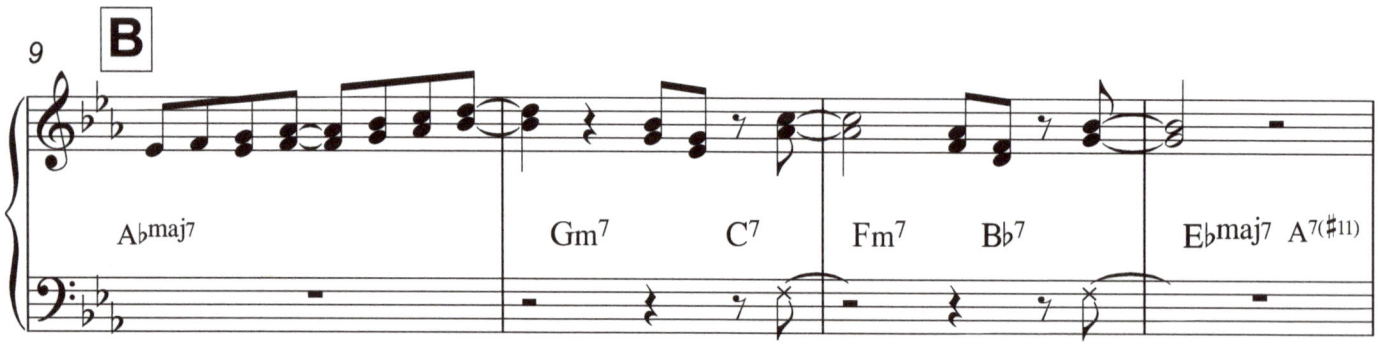

Venezuela

(Ganache dark chocolate)

Feelings, mood: Tranquility, safety, softness, generosity, confidence, protection.

Main ingredients: Santo Domingo 82% cocoa, cream from Bresse.

Sensory analysis: Real bitterness; a bit of astringency; some sweetness; dry fruits; notes of banana, nuts, almond and cream.

Global flavor: Power, character, authority, depth, harmony, energy.

Ciacca 5

Jazz in St. Germain Chocolate

Feelings, mood: Softness, lightness, delicacy.

"Global flavor": Softness, lightness, sensitivity, seduction, sensuality.

Jazz will be evoked by notes of whisky, cedar wood, and nutty flavors.

Petit Richart chocolate

(Passion fruit-mango emulsion)

Feelings, mood: Tonicity, vitality, excitement, ardor

Main ingredients: Mango pulp, 73% Venezuela cocoa, passion fruit pulp, Tahitian vanilla, cream, butter.

Sensory analysis: Balance between sweetness and acidity, fruity aromas, melting and tender texture, dairy aromas.

"Global flavor": Tonicity, vitality, excitement, ardor.

Besame Lucio

Medium " Boogaloo groove"

Music by Antonio Ciacca

22

7 Spice Chocomac

Feelings: Exoticism, difference, exuberance, travel, adventure.

Main ingredients: West Indies 75% cocoa, Cream from Bresse, Sweet spice infusion.

Sensory analysis: Balance of among sweet, sour, and bitter. Aromas of cardamom, coriander, star anise, nutmeg, ginger, vanilla, cinnamon, and cream.

"Global flavor": Exoticism, difference, exuberance, travel, adventure.

SCOTTY

Up tempo Latin/Swing

Antonio Ciacca

www.ingramcontent.com/pod-product-compliance
Lightning Source LLC
Chambersburg PA
CBHW042005150426
43194CB00002B/128